The Holy Typica
Deacon's Service

Sts. Simon & Jude Eastern Orthodox Church

This Service is used when there is no priest or cantor/reader

If no other Service had proceeded, all start with the Trishagion Prayers:

Deacon: **In the Name of the Father and of the Son and of the Holy Spirit. Amen. Glory to thee, our God, glory to thee.**

All: **O heavenly King, the comforter, the Spirit of truth, who art in all places and fillest all things; treasury of good things and giver of life: Come and dwell in us and cleanse us from every stain, and save our souls, O gracious Lord.**

Holy God, Holy Mighty, Holy Immortal: have mercy on us. *(Thrice)*

Glory to the Father and to the Son and to the Holy Spirit: now and ever and unto ages of ages. Amen.

All-holy Trinity, have mercy on us. Lord, cleanse us from our sins. Master, pardon our iniquities. Holy God, visit and heal our infirmities for thy Name's sake.

Lord, have mercy. *(3x)*

Glory to the Father and to the Son and to the

Holy Spirit: now and ever and unto ages of ages. Amen.

Our Father, who art in heaven, hallowed be thy Name; thy kingdom come; thy will be done on earth, as it is in heaven. Give us this day our daily bread; and forgive us our trespasses, as we forgive those who trespass against us; and lead us not into temptation, but deliver us from evil.

Through the prayers of our holy Fathers and Mothers, Lord Jesus Christ our God, have mercy on us and save us. Amen.

Through the prayers of our holy fathers and mothers, Lord Jesus Christ our God, have mercy upon us. Amen.

<h1 align="center">The First Antiphon</h1>

Psalm 102(103)

All: **Bless the Lord, O my soul. Blessed art Thou, O Lord.**

Bless the Lord, O my soul. And all that is within me, bless His holy Name.

Bless the Lord, O my soul. And forget not all His benefits.

Who forgives all your iniquities, who heals all your diseases.

The Lord is compassionate and merciful, long-suffering and of great goodness.

Bless the Lord, O my soul. Blessed art Thou, O Lord.

<h1 align="center">The Second Antiphon</h1>

Psalm 145(146)

Deacon/Reader: **Glory to the Father and to the Son and to the Holy Spirit.**

All: **Praise the Lord, O my soul. I will praise the Lord as long as I live;**

I will sing praises to my God while I have being.

Put not your trust in princes, in sons of men in whom there is no salvation.

When his breath departs he returns to his earth: on that very day his plans perish.

The Lord will reign forever; Thy God, O Zion, to all generations.

All: **Now and ever and unto ages of ages. Amen.**

Hymn
by Emperor Justinian I (527-565)

All: **Only-begotten Son and immortal Word of God, who for our salvation didst will to be incarnate of the holy Theotokos and Ever-Virgin Mary; who without change didst become man and was crucified. O Christ our God, trampling down death by death; who art one of the Holy Trinity, glorified with the Father and the Holy Spirit: Save us.**

The Third Antiphon
(The Beatitudes)

All: **In Thy Kingdom remember us, O Lord, when Thou comest in Thy Kingdom.**
Blessed are the poor in spirit, for theirs is the kingdom of heaven.
Blessed are those who mourn, for they shall be comforted.
Blessed are the meek, for they shall inherit the earth.
Blessed are those who hunger and thirst after righteousness, for they shall be filled.
Blessed are the merciful, for they shall obtain mercy.
Blessed are the pure in heart, for they shall see God.
Blessed are the peacemakers, for they shall be called the sons of God.
Blessed are they that are persecuted for righteousness sake, for theirs is the kingdom of heaven.

Blessed are you, when men shall revile you and persecute you and shall say all manner of evil against you falsely, for my sake.

Rejoice and be exceedingly glad, for great is your reward in heaven.

The Entrance Hymn

Come, let us worship and fall down before Christ, who didst rise from the dead,

O Son of God, save us who sing to Thee: Alleluia.

Now the Reader (or Deacon) chants or sings the Resurrectional Troparion and Kontakion in the tone of the week.

Resurrectional Troparion And Theotokion

First Tone

Though the tomb was sealed by a stone and soldiers guarded your pure body, yet you arose on the third day, giving life to the world. Therefore, O Giver of life, the heavenly powers praise you: Glory to your resurrection, O Christ! Glory to your kingdom! Glory to your plan of redemption, O only loving God.

At the sound of Gabriel's voice calling out to you: Hail, Virgin, the Master of all became incarnate in you, the holy Tabernacle as David the righteous said. By bearing your Creator, you have shown yourself to be more spacious than the heavens. Glory to him who dwelled in you! Glory to him who came forth from you! Glory to him who by your childbirth has set us free!

O life immortal, when you descended unto death, you destroyed Hades with the splendor of your divinity, and when you raised the dead from the depths of darkness, all the heavenly powers shouted: O Giver of life, Christ our God, glory to you.

Your mystery O Theotokos, is most glorious and surpasses all understanding. For sealed with purity and inviolate in virginity, you are acknowledged without doubt to be the mother who gave birth to the true God. Beseech him to save our souls.

Let the heavens rejoice and the earth be glad, for the Lord has shown the power of his reign: he has conquered death by death, and become the first born of the dead. He has delivered us from the depths of Hades, and has granted the world great mercy.

We sing your praise, O Virgin Theotokos. You intercede for the salvation of our race; for by taking flesh of you and by the cross, your Son and our God has delivered us from corruption as a loving God.

The joyful news of your resurrection was told to the women disciples of the Lord by the angel. And throwing off the ancestral curse, they boastingly told the Apostles: death has been vanquished, Christ our God is risen, bestowing great mercy on the world.

The mystery hidden from all ages and unknown to the angels was made manifest to those on earth through you, O Theotokos. God took flesh in a union without confusion, and for our sake he willingly accepted the cross. Thereby he raised the first-created man and saved our souls from death.

O faithful, let us give praise and worship to the Word, co-eternal with the Father and the Spirit, born of the Virgin for our salvation. Of his own will he mounted the cross in the flesh, suffered death, and raised the dead through his glorious resurrection.

Rejoice! Impassable gateway of the Lord. Rejoice! wall and protection of those who take refuge in you. Rejoice! you who have not known wedlock and have given birth to your Son and Maker and God in the flesh. Cease not in your intercession on behalf of those who praise and worship your Son.

The angelic powers appeared at your tomb, and those guarding it became as dead. Mary stood at your grave seeking your pure body. You stripped the power -of Hades, yet remained untouched by its corruption. You met the Virgin and bestowed life. O Lord, who rose from the dead, glory to you.

You called your mother blessed when you went of your own will to your passion shining upon the cross. Seeking Adam, you said to the angels: Rejoice with me, for the lost piece of silver has been found. O God, you have ordered all things wisely, glory to you.

Through your cross you destroyed death and opened paradise to the thief. You transformed the sorrow of the Myrrh-bearers, Christ our God. You commanded the apostles to proclaim that you have risen from the dead, and granted great mercy to the world.

You are praised by all the world, O Virgin, and are the treasure house of the resurrection. Lead those who have put their faith in you out of the pit and abyss of their offenses. Before bearing a child you were a virgin, and in childbirth and after childbirth you remained a virgin. By giving birth to salvation, you have saved us who were guilty of sin.

Eighth Tone

O merciful Lord, you descended from on high and endured the three-day burial to free us from our passions. O Lord, our life and resurrection, glory to you.

O good Lord, for our sake, you were born of a virgin and endured crucifixion, despoiling death by death, and, as God, you have shown forth the resurrection. Do not despise the work of your hands. Show your love for all, O merciful Lord. Accept the intercession made on our behalf by the Theotokos who gave birth to you, our Savior, to save your despairing people.

The Trisagion

People: **Holy God. Holy Mighty. Holy Immortal, have mercy on us.** *(3x)*

Glory to the Father, and to the Son, and to the Holy Spirit. Now and ever, and unto ages of ages. Amen.

Holy Immortal. Have mercy on us.

Holy God. Holy Mighty. Holy Immortal. Have mercy on us.

The Epistle Reading

Reader/Deacon: **The reading from the Epistle of St. Paul to the __________.**

People: Alleluia (3x)

The Gospel Reading

Some Orthodox jurisdictions require a specific blessing for a member of the laity to read the Gospel. If unsure, simply skip over the following.

Deacon: **The reading from the Holy Gospel according to St. __________.**
All: **Glory to Thee, O Lord, glory to Thee.**

Read (not chant) the Gospel from the center of the nave <u>facing the altar</u>.

When the Gospel reading is completed:
All: **Glory to Thee, O Lord, glory to Thee.**

If the Service is led by a Deacon or Deaconess, and he or she has the bishop's blessing to preach, it is given now.

The sermon can also be replaced by a section from spiritual literature, such as from the writings of the Holy Fathers.

Prayer To The Lord Of Hosts

Reader: **Glory to the Father and to the Son and to the Holy Spirit, now and ever and unto ages of ages. Amen.**

**Remember us, O Lord, when You come into Your Kingdom.
Remember us, O Master, when You come into Your Kingdom.
Remember us, O Holy One, when You come into Your Kingdom.**

**The heavenly choir sings to You and cries: Holy, Holy, Holy, Lord God of Hosts; heaven and earth are full of Your glory.
Come unto Him and be enlightened, and your faces shall not be ashamed.
The heavenly choir sings to You and cries: Holy, Holy, Holy, Lord God of Hosts; heaven and earth are full of Your glory.**

Glory to the Father and to the Son and to the Holy Spirit:

The choir of holy angels and archangels, with all the powers of heaven, sing Your praises and do cry: Holy, Holy, Holy, Lord God of Hosts; heaven and earth are full of Your glory.

Now and ever and unto ages of ages. Amen.

The Symbol of Faith

The decrees of the Ecumenical Councils at Nicaea (325) and Constantinople (381)

All: **I believe in one God, the Father Almighty, maker of heaven and earth, and of all things visible and invisible.**

I believe in one Lord Jesus Christ, the Son of God, the only-begotten, begotten of the Father before all ages.

Light of Light; true God of true God;

Begotten, not made; of one essence with the Father, by whom all things were made;

Who for us and for our salvation came down from heaven and was incarnate by the Holy Spirit and the Virgin Mary; and became man.

He was crucified for us under Pontius Pilate and suffered and was buried.

On the third day He rose again, according to the Scriptures, and ascended into heaven sitting at the right hand of the Father.

He shall come again with glory to judge the living and the dead; whose kingdom shall have no end.

I believe in the Holy Spirit, the Lord, the Giver of Life, who proceeds from the Father; who with the Father and the Son together is worshipped and glorified; who spoke by the prophets.

In one holy, universal and apostolic Church.

I acknowledge onc baptism for the remission of sins.

I look for the resurrection of the departed and the life of the world to come. Amen.

The Prayer Of Forgiveness

Deacon: **O God, remit, pardon and forgive our sins, whether voluntary or involuntary, whether by words or deeds, whether in knowledge or ignorance, whether by day or night, whether in mind or thought; forgive us all these, for You are good and loves humankind.**

The Lord's Prayer

All (spoken):
Our Father, who art in heaven,
hallowed be Thy name,
Thy Kingdom come.
Thy will be done, on earth as it is in heaven.
Give us this day our daily bread;
and forgive us our offences,
as we forgive those who have offended us;
and lead us not into temptation,
but deliver us from evil. Amen.

Theotokion
(Tone 6)

All: **Steadfast protectress of Christians, constant advocate before the creator: Despise not the entreating cries of us sinners, but in your goodness come speedily to those who call on you in faith. Hasten to hear our petition and to intercede for us, O Theotokos: For you always protect those who honor you.**

Reader: **All-holy Trinity, mighty one in essence, kingdom undivided, origin of all good things, be graciously inclined also to me, a sinner. Establish me; give understanding to my heart, and purge away all my vileness. Enlighten my mind that I may glorify, sing praises and adore You saying:**

All: **One is Holy, One is the Lord, Jesus Christ, in the glory of God the Father. Amen.**

Blessed be the name of the Lord, henceforth and forevermore. *(3x)*

17

Reader: **Glory to the Father and to the Son and to the Holy Spirit, now and ever and unto ages of ages. Amen.**

I will bless the Lord at all times; his praise shall continually be in my mouth. My soul makes its boast in the Lord; let the afflicted hear and be glad. O magnify the Lord with me, and let us exalt His name together. I sought the Lord, and he answered me. Look to Him, and be radiant; so your faces shall not be ashamed. This poor man cried, and the Lord heard him, and saved him out of all his troubles. The angel of the Lord encamps around those who fear Him, and delivers them. O taste and see that the Lord is good.

Happy is the man who takes refuge in Him. O fear the Lord, you His saints, for those who fear Him have no want. The young lions suffer want and hunger; but those who seek the Lord lack no good thing.

Come, O sons, listen to me, I will teach you the fear of the Lord. What man is there who desires life, and covets many days, that he may enjoy good? Keep your tongue from evil, and your lips from speaking deceit. Depart from evil, and do good; seek peace, and pursue it. The eyes of the Lord are toward the righteous, and his ears toward their cry. The face of the Lord is against evildoers, to cut off the remembrance of them from the earth. When the righteous cry for help,

the Lord hears, and delivers them out of all their troubles. The Lord is near to the brokenhearted, and saves the crushed in spirit. Many are the afflictions of the righteous; but the Lord delivers him out of them all. He kept all his bones; not one of them is broken. Evil shall slay the wicked; and those who hate the righteous will be condemned. The Lord redeems the life of his servants; none of those who take refuge in Him will be condemned.

Hymn To The Theotokos
(Tone 8)

All: It is truly meet to bless you, O Theotokos, ever blessed and most pure and the Mother of our God. More honorable than the Cherubim and more glorious beyond compare than the Seraphim: Without defilement you gave birth to God the Word, true Theotokos, we magnify you.

The Dismissal

All: **Glory to the Father and to the Son and to the Holy Spirit, now and ever and unto ages of ages. Amen. Lord, have mercy.** *(3x)*

Deacon: **Lord Jesus Christ, Son of God, through the prayers of Thy most pure mother; by the power of the honorable and life-giving cross; and by the holy bodiless powers of heaven; of our holy, venerable and God-bearing fathers; and of all Thy saints, have mercy on us.**

All: **Amen.**